THE BEGINNER'S GUIDE

DRAWING

CARTOONS

BY

PETER COUPE

ARCTURUS

015190

PUBLISHED BY ARCTURUS PUBLISHING LIMITED
FOR BOOKMART LIMITED
REGISTERED NUMBER - 2372865
TRADING AS BOOKMART LIMITED
DESFORD ROAD
ENDERBY
LEICESTER
LE9 5AD

THIS EDITION PUBLISHED - 2000

ISBN 1 84193 039 3

CONTENTS

HELLO ...

IN THIS BOOK I AM GOING TO SHOW YOU HOW TO DRAW CARTOONS. EVEN IF YOU HAVE NEVER DRAWN ANYTHING BEFORE - YOU CAN DRAW CARTOONS. ONCE YOU HAVE LEARNED THE BASICS THERE WILL BE NO STOPPING YOU!

* ALL YOU NEED TO START IS A PENCIL AND SOME PAPER.

ENTHUSIASM, YOU NEED SOME OF THIS TOO!

PENCIL →

PAPER

READY, SET, LET'S GO ...

LET'S START WITH SOMETHING THAT MOST OF US WILL HAVE DRAWN AT SOME TIME...
...STICK FIGURES!

AN OLD MASTERPIECE

← AN OLD MASTER

EVEN "REAL" ARTISTS WILL OFTEN START THEIR PAINTINGS WITH A STICK FIGURE SKETCH. IT HELPS THEM GET EVERYTHING IN ITS PLACE. IN FACT, THE WORD 'CARTOON' ORIGINALLY MEANT...

...A QUICK SKETCH FOR AN OIL PAINTING!

STICK FIGURES ARE REALLY EASY!

① DRAW A LOLLIPOP SHAPE...
THIS MAKES THE HEAD AND
THE BACKBONE...

② ...NOW ADD THE HIPS
AT THE BOTTOM OF
THE BACKBONE AND
SHOULDERS AT THE
TOP...

③ ...TWO ARMS NEXT-
FIXED AT THE ENDS
OF THE SHOULDERS...

④ NOW THE LEGS...

AND THAT'S IT!
YOUR VERY FIRST CARTOON!

* LEAVE OFF THE HIP AND SHOULDER
STICKS WHEN YOU DRAW A FIGURE
FROM THE SIDE — BECAUSE YOU CAN'T
SEE THEM.   CHECK THIS IN A MIRROR!

7

WE WANT PLENTY OF ACTION IN OUR CARTOONS –
SO LET'S DRAW OUR SIMPLE STICK FIGURES IN A
VARIETY OF DIFFERENT POSES...

SOMEONE RUNNING WILL
BE LEANING FORWARD,
LIKE THIS.

SOMEONE SITTING IN
A CHAIR WILL BE
LEANING BACK.

PUSHING A SUPERMARKET
TROLLY CAN BE HARD WORK...

KICKING A FOOTBALL
IS ENERGETIC...

NOT TO MENTION
DANCING A HIGHLAND
FLING!

YOU CAN MAKE A **REAL** STICK FIGURE TO HELP
WORK OUT SOME OF THESE POSES...

SPENT
MATCHES
ONLY!

USE SPENT MATCHES,
DRINKING STRAWS,
COCKTAIL STICKS OR
PENCILS. LAY THEM
OUT, THEN COPY THE
SHAPES ON TO PAPER.

USE LITTLE
STICKS FOR
FINGERS...
A BLOB
FOR THE
HEAD...
SIMPLE
SHAPES FOR
FEET.

YOU CAN ALSO USE SHAPES FROM
NEWSPAPERS...
USE TRACING PAPER TO
COPY FROM PHOTOGRAPHS.

TRACING
PAPER

NEWSPAPER

CARTOONIST

... NOW, WHICH
PAGE HAS THE
BIG MATCH
FEATURE?

9

THERE IS NOTHING TO STOP YOU MAKING ODD SHAPES
WITH YOUR STICK FIGURES...
YOU DON'T HAVE TO KEEP TO "NORMAL" PROPORTIONS.

LONG ARMS AND SHORT
LEGS MIGHT BE USEFUL
FOR A BASKETBALL
PLAYER.

OR - SHORT ARMS
AND LONG LEGS!

...MY HERO!
...SIGH!

REMEMBER...
STICKS FOR
FINGERS - BLOBS
FOR FEET.

BIG SHOULDERS
AND SMALL HIPS
FOR THAT...
SUPER HERO
LOOK!

CAPTAIN SHOULDERS

NOW YOU CAN START DRAWING YOUR VERY OWN CARTOONS USING THESE SIMPLE STICK FIGURES...

COME HERE - I NEED SOME STICKS TO MAKE A FIRE!

YOU CAN EVEN DRAW SIMPLE STRIP CARTOONS...

AAAAARRGGHH!

SPEND SOME TIME PRACTISING THESE BASIC STICK FIGURES—THEY WILL HELP YOU TO DRAW GOOD, ACTION PACKED CARTOONS!

WE'LL HAVE A BREAK FROM STICK FIGURES NOW. IN THE NEXT SECTION WE WILL LEARN TO DRAW...

FUNNY FACES!

MIRROR

IF YOU WANT TO SEE SOME FUNNY FACES TAKE A LOOK IN HERE!

ISLE COLLEGE
RESOURCES CENTRE

DRAWING FUNNY FACES...

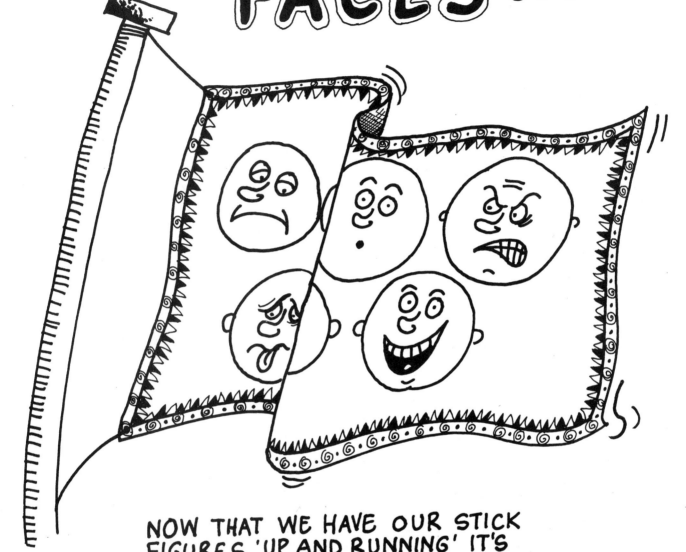

NOW THAT WE HAVE OUR STICK
FIGURES 'UP AND RUNNING' IT'S
TIME TO GIVE THEM PERSONALITIES
OF THEIR OWN...

...THE FACES IN CARTOONS ARE
IMPORTANT. THEY CONVEY THE
EMOTIONS YOUR CHARACTERS
ARE FEELING.

...COPY MY FACES TO BEGIN WITH -
YOU WILL SOON DEVELOP YOUR OWN.

DRAW THESE FACES IN SIMPLE
OVAL SHAPES – WITH AN
UPSIDE DOWN QUESTION MARK
FOR A NOSE, AND THE NUMBER
'3' FOR EARS.

IN A SURPRISED FACE ↗
THE EYES ARE DRAWN WIDE
OPEN, WITH THE EYEBROWS
HIGH IN THE FOREHEAD. THE
MOUTH IS JUST A LITTLE DOT.

IN A CONTENTED FACE
THE EYES AND MOUTH ARE
SIMPLE CURVES – FACING
UPWARDS.

* WE ALSO USE THIS FACE
FOR SOMEONE WHO IS
PROUD.

IN A SAD FACE WE REVERSE
ALL THE CURVES – THE
EYES AND MOUTH TURN
DOWN.

* MAKE A POINT OF LOOKING
AT LOTS OF CARTOONS TO
SEE HOW THE DIFFERENT
FACES ARE DRAWN!

IF WE USE THE EYES FROM THE SURPRISED FACE AND THE MOUTH FROM THE CONTENTED FACE WE HAVE A... HAPPY FACE...

... MAKE THE SMILE BIGGER - COMPLETE WITH TEETH - AND YOU HAVE A LOTTERY WINNER

AN ANGRY FACE LOOKS OUT FROM UNDER THESE DOWN POINTING EYEBROWS... ... COMPLETE WITH BARED TEETH !

SAY LENGRHH !

A SICK FACE HAS SAD EYES ~ AND A WIGGLY MOUTH.

* HAVE THE TONGUE STICKING OUT, OR A THERMOMETER, TO SHOW ILLNESS.

HE MUST BE THE LOTTERY LOSER !

WE HAVE NOW DRAWN THE SIX MOST COMMON FACES YOU WILL FIND IN CARTOONS.

ONCE YOU HAVE LEARNED THESE BASIC EXPRESSIONS YOU CAN CREATE NEW ONES OF YOUR OWN...

YOU CAN CREATE ANY NUMBER OF FACES BY COMBINING THE FEATURES YOU ALREADY KNOW...

PLOTTING REVENGE ↓

ANGRY EYES ✛ HAPPY MOUTH

MAKING THE BEST OF IT ↘

HAPPY EYES ✛ SAD MOUTH

OOPS! ↓

SAD EYES ✛ SURPRISED MOUTH

LEARN TO DRAW FACES FROM THE SIDE AS WELL AS THE FRONT...

...USE THE SAME SHAPE FOR THE NOSE...

...DRAW HALF THE MOUTH...

...MAKE THE EYE FURTHEST FROM YOU A BIT SMALLER.

DRAW YOUR OWN FACE WITH A MIRROR...

* ON THE NEXT PAGE WE'LL SEE HOW TO MAKE THESE FACES INTO MEN AND WOMEN.

16

IT'S EASY TO MAKE THESE SIMPLE FACES INTO MALE OR FEMALE CARTOON CHARACTERS...

WOMEN CAN HAVE LONG EYELASHES AND LIPSTICK... AND OFTEN HAVE MORE HAIR THAN MEN!

MEN CAN BE STUBBLY, WITH SHORT HAIR - OR EVEN NONE AT ALL!

DRAW A FEW SIMPLE FACES AND HAVE A GO...

* PICK UP YOUR PENCIL AND TRY IT!

SOME FACES CAN EITHER BE MALE OR FEMALE...

... LIKE THIS ONE

17

AS WELL AS BEING MALE OR FEMALE, YOUR CARTOON PEOPLE CAN BE YOUNG AND OLD...

... OLDIES - LIKE ME - OFTEN HAVE WRINKLES - AND MIGHT BE A LITTLE MORE STOOPED... THEY WILL ALSO DRESS IN A MORE CONSERVATIVE WAY. (NORMALLY!)

MUST BE PENSION DAY...

SUPER GRAMPS

IT'S ALSO LOTS OF FUN DRAWING YOUNG PEOPLE. THEY ARE THE ONES MOST LIKELY TO DRESS IN A CRAZY WAY TO BEGIN WITH!

VERY YOUNG CHILDREN HAVE LARGE HEADS AND SMALL BODIES.

YOU CAN –IF YOU WANT– ADD LOTS OF **DETAIL** TO YOUR CARTOONS...

...BEARDS AND MOUSTACHES
... SPECTACLES, HATS,
... PORTABLE STEREOS, ETC, ETC !

HUMF
WELL
HUMF
...

SSTTSS
SSSTTSS
SSSTTTSS
TTSSTSS

TSSSKK
TSSSKK

...MAKE YOUR CARTOONS ACTIVE BY ADDING BEADS OF SWEAT, SHAKE LINES AND EXTREME EXPRESSIONS!

...ON THE OTHER HAND – IF YOU WANT TO KEEP YOUR CARTOONS NICE AND SIMPLE...
...THAT'S FINE TOO!

GGRRR...
GGGRRR
GRRRR
...

TUT
TUT
TUT....

* OF COURSE, YOUR CARTOON CHARACTER DOESN'T HAVE TO BE A PERSON... ➔

19

FOR EXAMPLE ... **ANIMALS ...**

... ARE LOTS OF FUN TO DRAW AND APPEAL TO ALMOST EVERYONE. EITHER SOFT AND CUDDLY, OR PLENTY OF WHISKERS, FUR AND SHARP TEETH ...!

* AS WELL AS ANIMALS, WHY NOT TRY SOME TALKING SHOES-A SINGING CAMERA OR A COMPUTER THAT TYPES YOUR LETTERS FOR YOU?

YOU CAN BRING ALMOST ANYTHING TO LIFE!

NOW YOU CAN COMBINE THE **FUNNY FACES** WITH THE STICK FIGURES FROM THE LAST SECTION ...

.... YOUR CARTOONS WILL REALLY START TO COME TO LIFE NOW **!**

SO FAR WE HAVE ONLY BEEN DRAWING IN PENCIL;
AS YOU BECOME MORE CONFIDENT YOU WILL WANT
TO MAKE YOUR DRAWING MORE PERMANENT.

THIS IS WHAT I USE ...

PENCIL - USED FOR GENERAL
SKETCHING AND ROUGH LAYOUTS.
A GRADE 'B' IS EASY TO RUB OUT.

TECHNICAL PEN -
GIVES A VERY EVEN AND
PRECISE LINE. THIS BOOK
WAS DRAWN AND LETTERED
WITH A TECHNICAL PEN!

FOUNTAIN PEN -
USE A WATER BASED INK IN A
FOUNTAIN PEN OR IT MAY CLOG.
OLD 'DIP' PENS ARE ALSO FUN
TO EXPERIMENT WITH.

FELT-TIPPED PENS -
ARE CHEAP AND EASY TO REFILL.
THE INK CAN FADE IN TIME, SO
USE FOR SKETCHES ONLY!

*
I USUALLY DRAW MY CARTOONS IN
PENCIL FIRST. THEN I DRAW OVER
IT WITH A TECHNICAL PEN. WHEN THE
INK IS COMPLETELY DRY I RUB OUT
THE PENCIL LINES.

SOME CARTOONISTS DRAW
WITH A BRUSH -
YOU COULD TRY
THIS YOURSELF.

23

TO KEEP YOUR PENCILS AT THEIR BEST YOU WILL NEED A PENCIL SHARPENER.

A SOFT RUBBER WILL REMOVE UNWANTED PENCIL LINES WITHOUT DAMAGING THE PAPER.

COVER UP SMALL MISTAKES WITH TYPEWRITER CORRECTION FLUID.

COVER UP LARGER MISTAKES WITH A 'GLUED ON' PATCH OF PAPER – THEN SIMPLY REDRAW OVER THIS.

* IT'S O.K. – LOTS OF FAMOUS CARTOONISTS HAVE TO PATCH AND CORRECT !

HELLO... PATCH

....AND NOW→LET'S LEARN TO DRAW...

HANDS

AND

FEET.

* YOU CAN HAVE EVEN MORE FUN WITH YOUR CARTOON CHARACTERS ONCE THEY HAVE HANDS AND FEET.
OVER THE NEXT FEW PAGES I WILL SHOW YOU SOME SIMPLE WAYS TO DRAW THESE ESSENTIAL EXTREMITIES...

...NOW... BEST **FEET** FORWARD...

START OUT BY DRAWING REALLY SIMPLE SHAPES FOR FEET — LIKE THESE...

ALWAYS DRAW SOME SORT OF **HEEL** SHAPE AT THE BACK — IT HELPS TO BALANCE THE FOOT.

* THE BIG TOE POINTS UP THE OTHERS POINT DOWN.

EXPERIMENT WITH BARE FEET, BOOTS, SHOES, SLIPPERS, CLAWS ?!*.?

MEN...

MAINLY WEAR FLAT-SOLED SHOES AND BOOTS.

THEY OFTEN HAVE HAIRY FEET.

TRY DRAWING SLIPPERS, WELLIES, SANDALS, HIKING BOOTS AND CRAZY TRAINERS!

WOMEN...

...OFTEN WEAR A WIDER VARIETY OF MUCH MORE INTERESTING FOOTWEAR.

...EVERYTHING THAT MEN WEAR PLUS HIGH HEELS, SLINKY BOOTS AND FURRY SLIPPERS.

LET YOURSELF GO!

REMEMBER— THE HEEL HELPS BALANCE THE FOOT!

NOW – LET'S ADD SOME FEET AND SHOES TO OUR STICK FIGURES.

* PRACTISE A FEW OF THESE – BUILD YOUR CONFIDENCE!

YiKE! TRAINERS

* IN THESE CARTOONS THE HANDS PLAY AN IMPORTANT PART IN MAKING THE JOKE —

SO — TURN THE PAGE AND WE'LL LEARN HOW TO DRAW THEM !

HANDS ARE IMPORTANT IN CARTOONS.

THEY CAN GRIP, POINT, SQUEEZE, WAVE, THREATEN, THROW AND MUCH, MUCH MORE!

A SIMPLE HAND CAN BE DRAWN QUICKLY - LIKE A BUNCH OF BANANAS.

KEEP THE SHAPES SIMPLE AND DON'T WORRY ABOUT DETAILS.

"THROW"

GRIP

* FINGERS CAN BE ROUNDED OR SHARP, WRINKLED OR SMOOTH...

DON'T BOTHER WITH FINGERNAILS...

POINT

WAVE

3 FINGERS...

CARTOON HANDS CAN BE DRAWN WITH 3 FINGERS OR WITH 4 FINGERS — PICK THE ONE THAT SUITS YOU BEST!

LOVE + PEACE...

4 FINGERS

* TO GET THE THUMB IN THE RIGHT PLACE CHECK IN A MIRROR AS YOU DRAW.

HALT!

* MAKE THE HAND AS BIG AS YOU LIKE....

POP

DONE SOME ? DO SOME MORE!

OUR CARTOON FIGURE IS ALMOST COMPLETE...

...ALL WE HAVE TO DO NOW IS DRESS IT UP!

WE'VE DRAWN FUNNY FACES.

WE LEARNED TO DRAW HANDS.

WE'VE COVERED FEET AND SHOES.

WATCH THIS SPACE

IT'S NOT THE KIND OF SPACE I USUALLY WATCH— BUT I'LL GIVE IT A TRY!

YOU'VE BEEN WORKING HARD! HERE'S A 'CARTOON BREAK' BEFORE WE MOVE ON TO THE NEXT SECTION...

* LOOK AT THE HANDS - HOLDING AND COVERING THE 'PHONE!

THEATRICAL MANAGERS

" THEY NEED A DOUBLE ACT - CAN YOU CALL THE POT ?!"

* AS I SAID EARLIER, YOUR CARTOONS CAN BE ABOUT ANYTHING - EVEN KETTLES!

THE CLOTHES SHOW ...

BEGIN WITH THE USUAL STICK FIGURE — DRAWN IN SOFT PENCIL. A GRADE 'B' OR '2B' WILL ALLOW US TO RUB OUT THE PENCIL LINES EASILY WHEN THEY HAVE SERVED THEIR PURPOSE.

OVER THE STICK FIGURE CONSTRUCT A MORE ROUNDED FORM — USING 'BLOBS' FOR THE BODY AND TUBES FOR THE ARMS AND LEGS.

* ON THIS SIDE YOU CAN SEE THE 'BLOBS' AND 'TUBES' I USED TO HELP ME CONSTRUCT THIS FIGURE

ON THIS SIDE IS THE COMPLETED CARTOON FIGURE.

* COVER UP EACH SIDE WITH YOUR HAND TO SEE HOW ONE LEADS TO THE OTHER.

YOU CAN TRACE 'BLOB AND TUBE' FIGURES FROM NEWSPAPERS AND PHOTOGRAPHS AS WELL AS MAKING THEM FROM YOUR MATCHSTICK FIGURES.

EXPERIMENT WITH DIFFERENT PROPORTIONS...

SKETCHY 'BLOB' FIGURES

FINISHED CARTOON FIGURES

*USE A SOFT PENCIL FIRST. RUB OUT THE LINES WHEN THE INK IS COMPLETELY DRY.

→ KEEP A SMALL SKETCHPAD OR NOTEBOOK HANDY SO YOU CAN PRACTISE YOUR DRAWING WHENEVER THE MOOD TAKES YOU!

TRY DRAWING **MEN** IN SUITS, SHIRTS AND TIES, WOOLLY JUMPERS, HIKING GEAR, SCUBA DIVING SUITS, SWEATSHIRTS...

* COLLECT PICTURES FROM MAGAZINES FOR IDEAS.

MeN!

EXTRA LARGE

THE CLOTHING CAN BE PART OF THE CARTOON TOO! A SHIRT CAN FIT A LITTLE TOO SNUGLY, OR BE MORE THAN A LITTLE ON THE BAGGY SIDE!

WOMEN CAN - OF COURSE - WEAR ALL THE THINGS THAT MEN CAN, PLUS SKIRTS AND DRESSES TOO!

JO'S GARAGE

* DON'T WORRY ABOUT DRAWING 'PROPER' ARMS AND LEGS — JUST DRAW STICK SHAPES FOR NOW.

OF COURSE YOU DON'T HAVE TO STICK RIGIDLY TO ANY OF THESE CATEGORIES...

...JUST DO YOUR OWN THING!

* KEEP YOUR EYES OPEN FOR CHANGING STYLES AND FASHIONS – ESPECIALLY IF YOU ARE DRAWING YOUNG PEOPLE...

* WATCH OUT FOR REVIVALS...

THERE WAS NO SUCH THING AS FASHION WHEN I WAS A LAD!

*REMEMBER AS WELL ALL THOSE LITTLE EXTRAS THAT PEOPLE CARRY AROUND...

*TELEPHONES
BRIEFCASES
HANDBAGS
BROLLIES
STEREOS + C.D.s
etc, etc...

* SOME PEOPLE WEAR A UNIFORM...

* THAT'S WHY HE WEARS THAT MASK!

I BORROW THINGS AND PASS THEM ON TO OTHER PEOPLE... I'M A "LOAN ARRANGER"

SWAG

* BUILD UP A COLLECTION OF DRAWINGS FOR FUTURE REFERENCE.

43

LET YOUR CARTOONS SET YOU FREE!

* YOU DON'T **HAVE TO**
DRAW **CARTOONS**
ABOUT THE **PRESENT**
DAY – YOU CAN SETTLE
IN ANY PLACE AND
ANY TIME **YOU CHOOSE!**

* YOU CAN SET YOUR
CARTOONS ON
ANOTHER PLANET
IF **YOU** WANT TO...

→LET YOUR IMAGINATION RUN WILD... **WHY NOT?!***

44

JUST REMEMBER.. I GAVE ONE OF MY BEST RIBS FOR YOU!

ONE OF MY FIRST CARTOON STRIPS WAS SET IN THE...

GARDEN OF EDEN!

* WHY NOT TRY OUT YOUR FAVOURITE PERIOD IN HISTORY...

...FROM CAVE MEN (AND WOMEN) TO COMPUTERS - FROM STONEHENGE TO THE SPACE SHUTTLE.

- GO FOR IT!

* YOU ALSO HAVE THE WORLD OF THE IMAGINARY TO HAVE FUN WITH!

IF THEY CAN MAKE A WOMAN FROM A MAN'S RIB.....

"THIS IS MONSTROUS."

HOSPITAL BILL

..WHY ON EARTH DO THEY KEEP ALL THE LEFTOVERS?

BACKGROUNDS

AND

LOCATIONS

HERE IS A DRAWING OF **ME** IN MY
USUAL LOCATION...

...AT WORK IN
MY STUDIO.

* PENS
PENCILS
RADIO
BOOKS
TABLE
CHAIR
PAPER
DRAWING BOARD...

* I HAVEN'T INCLUDED EVERY SINGLE
THING FROM MY STUDIO IN MY
DRAWING — JUST ENOUGH TO SHOW
WHERE I AM — BUT NOT SO MUCH THAT
THE DRAWING BECOMES CLUTTERED.

MAKE A NOTE OF THE THINGS YOU SEE IN A PARTICULAR PLACE, THEN DRAW 3 OR 4 OF THEM...

... IT'S SURPRISING JUST HOW LITTLE YOU NEED TO SEE IN A DRAWING TO TELL YOU WHERE YOU ARE...

... USING THE COLLECTION OF SKETCHES ABOVE I MADE UP THIS PUB SCENE

*TRY IT YOURSELF!

* SPEND A FEW MINUTES SKETCHING "EVERYDAY" OBJECTS AS YOU MOVE FROM ONE PLACE TO ANOTHER.

NOTE DOWN ANY DETAILS THAT INTEREST YOU!

...THIS WAY YOUR SKETCHBOOK WILL BE FULL OF POTENTIAL IDEAS -**PLUS**- YOU WILL BE GETTING IN PLENTY OF DRAWING PRACTISE **!**

(BETTER THAN GETTING SQUARE EYES WATCHING TELEVISION)

* BEGIN BY SKETCHING THE THINGS YOU FIND IN ALL THE DIFFERENT ROOMS IN YOUR OWN HOME...

TELEVISION
VIDEO
PLANTS
BOOKS
LIGHTS
ETC,
ETC...

49

✳ HERE ARE ANOTHER TWO EXAMPLES...

...SEE HOW **LITTLE** YOU ACTUALLY NEED TO DRAW TO SET THE SCENE...

...PEOPLE IN UNIFORM ARE VERY USEFUL CLUES TO TELL THE "VIEWER" WHERE THE CARTOON IS SET.

✳ MANY 'PROFESSIONAL' PEOPLE...

...DOCTORS DENTISTS ARCHITECTS ETC...

...DISPLAY THEIR CERTIFICATES IN FRAMES...

...THIS IS ANOTHER GOOD 'CLUE' YOU CAN INCLUDE IN YOUR CARTOON.

50

YOU CAN HAVE A LOT OF FUN
EXPERIMENTING WITH
DIFFERENT VIEWPOINTS...

... LOOKING FROM BELOW
THINGS APPEAR AS IF
THE VIEWER WAS A
CHILD OR SMALL ANIMAL —
OR SOMEONE LYING
DOWN — WHICH IS THE
BEST WAY TO SKETCH IT!

* LOOKING FROM ABOVE
THE OPPOSITE HAPPENS —
YOU GET A 'BIRDS EYE VIEW'
OF THE WORLD.

→ STAND ON A CHAIR AND
SEE FOR YOURSELF!

* LIGHTLY PENCIL IN A TRIANGLE
SHAPE TO BEGIN WITH, AND
DRAW INSIDE IT.

51

DRAWING TECHNIQUES

NOW THAT YOU ARE DRAWING WITH A BIT MORE CONFIDENCE WE CAN TRY OUT SOME THINGS THAT WILL MAKE YOUR **CARTOONS** EVEN MORE GOOD LOOKING...

NIB

USE AREAS OF SOLID BLACK IN YOUR CARTOONS TO MAKE THEM STRONGER...
...IT CAN ALSO BE USED TO MAKE LIGHTER AREAS MORE IMPORTANT.

* USE **BLACK** INDIAN INK - APPLIED WITH A SIZE 3 OR 4 ARTISTS' BRUSH.

(WASH THE BRUSH OUT IN WARM, SOAPY WATER AFTER USE.)

* SOME CARTOONISTS ONLY EVER DRAW WITH A BRUSH - NEVER A PEN.

* FOR A COMPLETE CHANGE TRY DRAWING IN WHITE ON A BLACK BACKGROUND...

...TYPEWRITER CORRECTION FLUID WORKS WELL.

ADDING PATTERNS, SHADING OR TONE TO YOUR CARTOONS WILL MAKE THEM LOOK MORE 'FINISHED' AND LESS SKETCHY...

PATTERN + SHADING.

...TRY SOME OF THE PATTERNS ON PAGE 53 TO START YOU OFF —

—THEN INVENT SOME OF YOUR OWN!

* THE PATTERN YOU DRAW ON THINGS CAN HAVE QUITE A DRAMATIC EFFECT—

BE CAREFUL !

HELLO...

WHAT THE...

NOW... THAT'S FAR **ENOUGH!**

* TRY TARTAN —HERRINGBONE — AND OTHERS!

* IN A CARTOON WHICH CONTAINS A LOT OF DETAIL YOU CAN MAKE THE IMPORTANT PARTS STAND OUT BY DRAWING THEM WITH A THICKER LINE...

... THIS IS A GOOD TECHNIQUE TO LEARN - YOU CAN USE IT A LOT.

* I USE A •4 TECHNICAL PEN FOR THE FINE LINES...

* TRY DRAWING THIS THICKER LINE WITH A SIZE 3 OR 4 BRUSH.

* USE THE THINNER LINE TO ADD DETAILS - LIKE THE GIRL'S HAIR IN THE CARTOON ABOVE...

*YOU CAN -OF COURSE- DRAW YOUR CARTOONS WITH JUST ABOUT ANYTHING THAT YOU HAPPEN TO HAVE AROUND.

I'VE DRAWN THE TOP PART OF THIS FIGURE WITH A **TECHNICAL PEN**...

...THE BACKGROUND IS **FINGERTIPS** DIPPED IN INDIAN INK...

...THE NEXT SECTION IS DRAWN WITH A NUMBER 3 **BRUSH**...

... A HOME-MADE **QUILL PEN** WAS USED FOR THIS PART OF THE DRAWING -JUST CUT THE END OF THE QUILL INTO A ROUGH PEN NIB SHAPE...

... THE BOTTOM PART WAS DRAWN WITH A THICK **FELT-TIP PEN.** THE BACKGROUND IS A **SPONGE** DIPPED IN INK...

...THE LEGS **ARE SHADED WITH DOTS!**

TIME...

FOR ANOTHER **CARTOON** BREAK...

WELL — OTHER BOSSES MARRY SECRETARIES!

* **COMPARE** THESE TWO CARTOONS...

... THE TOP ONE HAS PLENTY OF **TONE + TEXTURE**...

... THE BOTTOM ONE IS A SIMPLE LINE DRAWING.

... SO, I'M STUCK WITH THIS PONY TAIL FOR THE REST OF ETERNITY ?!

HOPEFULLY, BY NOW, YOU WILL BE FINDING THE **ACTUAL DRAWING** OF YOUR CARTOONS A BIT EASIER.

SO-NOW WE NEED A GOOD SUPPLY OF **JOKE** IDEAS TO GIVE US SOMETHING TO DRAW...

... BECAUSE YOU NEVER KNOW WHERE YOUR CARTOONS WILL END UP!

FAME

HA HA HA HA HA

* ON THE NEXT FEW PAGES I WILL SHOW YOU MY METHODS OF "JOKE PRODUCTION"...

... WHEN YOU'VE READ THIS SECTION WHY NOT HAVE A TRY YOURSELF!?

WHERE DO YOU GET YOUR IDEAS ?

* CARTOON IDEAS ARE ALL AROUND US...

... YOU HAVE TO LEARN TO "TUNE IN" YOUR MIND TO PICK THEM UP...

* LISTEN TO FUNNY RADIO PROGRAMMES.
* ASK FAMILY AND FRIENDS TO TELL YOU THEIR FAVOURITE JOKES.
* WATCH TELEVISION.

'HERE'S A GOOD ONE...

'LISTEN TO THIS...'

'HAVE YOU HEARD THE ONE ABOUT...

'SO I SAID...

* TURN EXISTING JOKES ON THEIR HEADS - CHANGE THE CHARACTERS AROUND.
USE COMMON THEMES OR SITUATIONS...
THERE MUST BE THOUSANDS OF DESERT ISLAND CARTOONS!

THERE ARE OFTEN FUNNY 'SNIPPETS' IN NEWSPAPERS AND MAGAZINES...

... BUT WATCH OUT FOR THINGS HAPPENING BEHIND YOU WHILE YOU ARE READING!

* **WRITE DOWN** THE 'PUNCHLINE' TO A FAVOURITE JOKE OR CARTOON – THEN THINK UP YOUR OWN ORIGINAL DRAWING TO GO WITH IT.

* WE ARE NEVER VERY FAR FROM SIGNS AND NOTICES – WRITE A FEW OF YOUR OWN!

* JUST DRAW A COUPLE OF CHARACTERS DOING SOMETHING – AND SEE IF AN IDEA SPRINGS TO MIND. I OFTEN WORK LIKE THIS WHEN I GET STUCK FOR IDEAS.

PRETENDING NOT TO SEE THE **CASH** ONLY SIGN

REMEMBER... IF YOU CAN HAVE ONE IDEA, YOU CAN HAVE TEN; AND IF YOU CAN HAVE TEN IDEAS YOU COULD PRETTY SOON HAVE **HUNDREDS!!**

CONTRASTS... CAN BE FUNNY.

- ... OLD AND NEW
- ... FAST AND SLOW
- ... SMALL AND LARGE.

* **LAUREL AND HARDY** WERE FUNNY EVEN BEFORE THEY SAID OR DID ANYTHING BECAUSE OF THE CONTRAST IN THEIR SIZE AND SHAPE.

* TALL AND SHORT
- ... WET AND DRY
- ... STRONG AND WEAK

CHUG CHUG

* CONTRAST THE WAY THAT DIFFERENT CHARACTERS REACT IN A VARIETY OF SITUATIONS.

5000 YEAR OLD VASE

OOPS!

5000 YEAR OLD VASE.

CRASH TINKLE

5000

GOOD JOB IT WASN'T A NEW ONE!

PEOPLE HAVE JOBS, HOBBIES AND LEISURE INTERESTS THAT SOMETIMES INVOLVE USING SPECIALIST EQUIPMENT AND TERMS OR 'JARGON'.

SOME OF THESE THINGS CAN BE USED IN CARTOONS...

SKATEBOARDING...

PHOTOGRAPHY

DARTS

STEAM RADIO AND 'HAM' RADIO

* **IN SOME CARTOONS** THERE ARE THINGS WHICH ARE HIDDEN FROM ONE OR MORE OF THE CHARACTERS — THE JOKE IS IN THE FACT THAT YOU KNOW SOMETHING THAT PEOPLE IN THE CARTOON DON'T !

SNIFF SNIFF...

* SOMETIMES THE JOKE IS IN THE VERY END OF THE CAPTION OR 'PUNCHLINE'!

I THINK LOVE IS THE MOST IMPORTANT THING IN A RELATIONSHIP...

SO — I'VE DECIDED TO FALL IN LOVE WITH THE FIRST LOTTERY WINNER I MEET!

→ NOW, TRY A FEW OF THESE 'JOKE PRODUCTION' IDEAS FOR YOURSELF...

TIME FOR ANOTHER...

CARTOON BREAK!

FLAMIN' TOURISTS!

18 HOLES IN ONE - AS USUAL!

OFFICE PARTIES P.L.C.

IN   OUT   IN   OUT   SHAKE IT ALL ABOUT!

* SOME CARTOONS HAVE WORDS IN THEM — THERE ARE A VARIETY OF WAYS OF ADDING THESE WORDS TO YOUR DRAWING...

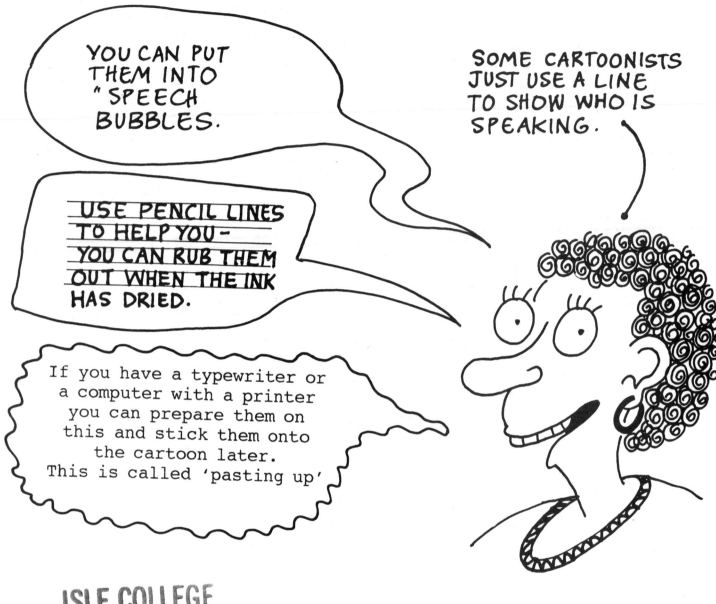

YOU CAN PUT THEM INTO "SPEECH BUBBLES.

USE PENCIL LINES TO HELP YOU — YOU CAN RUB THEM OUT WHEN THE INK HAS DRIED.

If you have a typewriter or a computer with a printer you can prepare them on this and stick them onto the cartoon later. This is called 'pasting up'

SOME CARTOONISTS JUST USE A LINE TO SHOW WHO IS SPEAKING.

MAKE SURE

THAT THE SPACES YOU LEAVE TO FIT THE WORDS INTO

ARE THE RIGHT SIZE!

AS WELL AS SPEECH
WE CAN ALSO ADD SOME
OF THESE TO OUR
CARTOONS . . .

"THINK" BUBBLES
ARE DRAWN **SOFT**
AND **FLUFFY**. . .

* **ANGRY OR EXPLOSIVE**
ACTIONS AND WORDS
ARE SHOWN IN **SPIKY**
SHAPES. . .

LIKE THIS!

* DIRECTIONS —OR GENERAL INFORMATION
FOR THE READER—IS USUALLY PUT INTO
RECTANGLES, LIKE THIS. . .

THE NEXT DAY. . .

→NOT ALL CARTOONS HAVE WORDS IN THEM —
SOME ARE PURELY "VISUAL" . . .

RESTAURANT de PARIS

AU REVOIR

WE SERVE SNAILS

* IN A 'VISUAL' **CARTOON** WE RELY ON THE DRAWING TO TELL THE WHOLE STORY.

THIS STYLE OF CARTOON CAN BE QUITE DIFFICULT TO "GET INTO" AT FIRST – TRY INCORPORATING SOME **SIGNS** TO BEGIN WITH, LIKE THE ONES I HAVE USED IN THE **CARTOON** AT THE TOP OF THIS PAGE.

DRAWING **CARICATURES**

CAN BE A LOT OF FUN, ESPECIALLY IF YOU HAVE A GIFT FOR IT!

*POLITICIANS, SUPERMODELS, ACTORS, ROYALS, MUSICIANS, ETC. ETC.

GET HOLD OF A **MIRROR** AND TRY IT OUT ON **YOURSELF** FIRST — OR WORK FROM **PHOTOS** OF FRIENDS AND FAMILY.

* THIS IS AN EXAMPLE OF HOW ONE OF MY CARTOONS LOOKS WHEN IT GOES OUT TO A NEWSPAPER OR MAGAZINE... ACTUAL SIZE! THE PRINTER WILL REDUCE IT TO THE SIZE REQUIRED BY THE MAGAZINE, LEAVING YOU FREE TO DRAW ANY SIZE YOU LIKE (ALMOST!).

You said take the baby to the park - you didn't say anything about bringing it back again...

* IF YOU'VE BEEN **WORKING HARD** YOUR CARTOONS WILL BE LOOKING PRETTY GOOD BY THIS STAGE.

MAYBE NOW IS THE TIME TO LET SOME OTHER PEOPLE ENJOY THEM...

WELL - WHAT DO YOU THINK?

BE HONEST...

...ER...

...WELL?

NERVOUS QUIVER.

➡ HERE ARE SOME IDEAS FOR THINGS YOU CAN DO WITH YOUR NEW-FOUND SKILLS...

✳ MAKE A FACE FOLDER!

TAKE A PIECE OF PAPER ABOUT
450mm BY 150mm.
FOLD IT INTO THREE EQUAL PARTS.
DRAW A FACE ON THE MIDDLE, THEN
FOLD EACH FLAP TO THE CENTRE AND
DRAW FACES ON THEM TOO.

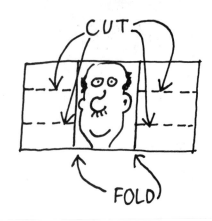

NOW CUT THE SIDE FLAPS INTO THREE STRIPS -
EACH ONE 50mm WIDE.

NOW YOU CAN CREATE AN **AMAZING ASSORTMENT**
OF FACES BY FOLDING AND UNFOLDING THE FLAPS.

✳ DRAW EYES IN THE TOP THIRD,
NOSE AND EARS IN THE SECOND THIRD,
MOUTH IN THE BOTTOM THIRD.

✳ MAKE THE FACES AS **VARIED** AS POSSIBLE.
MIX UP MALE AND FEMALE FACES.
ADD SOME **COLOUR** WITH PAINTS OR FELT PENS.

* WHY NOT **MAKE** YOUR **CHRISTMAS CARD** THIS YEAR?

1. DIVIDE AN **A4** SHEET INTO 4 EQUAL PARTS.

2. ADD YOUR CARTOON AND GREETING — NOTE THE LAYOUT SHOWN BELOW AND COPY IT **EXACTLY!**

3. PHOTOCOPY — FOLD ALONG THE DOTTED LINES — **SEND!**

I LOVE A TRADITIONAL **VICTORIAN** CHRISTMAS — ONE PENNY A CARD AND **NO MORE!**

MAKE AN INVITATION ...

* THE NEXT TIME YOU HAVE A PARTY WHY NOT SEND OUT YOUR OWN SPECIAL INVITATIONS...

... DRAW THEM ON PLAIN PAPER AND HAVE THEM PHOTOCOPIED.

... ADD SPOTS OF COLOUR.

... ABOVE ALL - MAKE THEM FUNNY.

IF YOU WANT TO SEE YOUR CARTOONS 'COME TO LIFE' WHY NOT MAKE A...

FLICKER BOOK ?!

* DRAW A SIMPLE STICK FIGURE ON THE LAST PAGE OF AN OLD NOTEPAD. ON THE PAGE BEFORE DRAW THE FIGURE AGAIN - BUT THIS TIME CHANGE IT SLIGHTLY. GO BACK ANOTHER PAGE AND DRAW ANOTHER - SLIGHTLY CHANGED - VERSION OF THE FIGURE.
   WHEN YOU HAVE DRAWN 20 'FRAMES' FLICK THE PAGES WITH YOUR THUMB!

* IF A WHOLE FIGURE IS TOO MUCH TRY SOMETHING SIMPLE - LIKE THIS BOUNCING BALL !

(NOTICE HOW THE BALL FLATTENS A LITTLE WHEN IT HITS THE GROUND)

TRAVELLING DOWN

THERE WILL BE TIMES WHEN YOU FIND YOURSELF WITH NO IDEAS AT ALL!
DON'T WORRY – IT HAPPENS TO ALL OF US!

OVER THE NEXT THREE PAGES I WILL REVEAL THE **SECRETS** OF...

... ➜ CREATIVE DOODLING!

✳ DRAW SOME LETTER AND NUMBER SHAPES AND USE THESE AS A STARTING POINT FOR A SKETCH...

NUMBER 6

NUMBER 5

LETTER G

LETTER

HERE ARE SOME READY-TO-USE **PUNCHLINES**! THINK UP SOME SUITABLY FUNNY DRAWINGS TO GO WITH THEM...

* 'HAVE YOU SEEN MY CAR KEYS ANYWHERE?'

* WHAT TIME DO YOU CALL THIS?

* JUST A QUICK ONE - THEN I REALLY MUST BE GOING!

* YOU'LL HAVE TO TRY MUCH HARDER THAN **THAT**!

* THERE WAS NOTHING IN THE INSTRUCTIONS ABOUT INSURANCE.

* FORE!

* DO YOU REALLY LOVE ME, SID?

* WHEN I NOD MY HEAD, YOU HIT IT!

* WELL - I'VE SEEN ENOUGH - HOW ABOUT YOU?

* PLEASE SEND ME A TELEPHONE DIRECTORY.

* IT'S FOR YOU.

* TAKE US TO YOUR LEADER...

* NOT ANOTHER ONE!

* YOU CALL **THAT** A COMPANY CAR?!

* APPARENTLY THAT IS CAUSED BY GLOBAL WARMING.

* I SEE THAT BENSON HAS OVERCOME HIS FEAR OF FLYING.

* AREN'T THEY NORMALLY SMALLER THAN THAT?

* ARE YOU SURE THIS IS AN OPTICIANS?

* THEY SAY IT'S EVEN MORE POPULAR THAN FOOTBALL.

AND FINALLY...

* HE WANTED TO BE A CARTOONIST - NOW LOOK AT HIM!

I HAVE STARTED THESE DRAWINGS—NOW YOU **FINISH** THEM...

YOU ONLY NEED **ONE** MORE THING TO GET YOUR
CARTOON DRAWING OFF TO A FLYING START...

...PRACTISE!

3.2.1...

* IF YOU CAN SET ASIDE
TEN OR FIFTEEN MINUTES
A DAY FOR CARTOON DRAWING
YOU WILL VERY QUICKLY SEE
YOUR ABILITIES GROW!

MAKE SURE...

   ... YOU WORK IN A **COMFORTABLE** PLACE.

   ... YOUR **EQUIPMENT** IS READY BEFORE YOU
     START.

   ... YOU HAVE PLENTY OF **LIGHT** - SO YOU
     CAN SEE WHAT YOU ARE DOING.

   ... YOU **ENJOY** YOUR CARTOONING!
     (IF YOU'RE NOT IN THE MOOD - LEAVE
     IT UNTIL YOU ARE).

* GIVE YOURSELF A LITTLE **REWARD** WHENEVER
YOU LEARN SOMETHING **NEW**!

WELL - THAT BRINGS US TO THE END OF OUR BEGINNER'S GUIDE TO DRAWING CARTOONS.

I HOPE YOU HAVE ENJOYED THIS BOOK, AND I HOPE YOU HAVE BEEN INSPIRED TO PICK UP A PEN OR PENCIL AND HAVE A GO FOR YOURSELF!

HAPPY CARTOONING!

As well as writing books *Peter Coupe* also runs a cartoon drawing correspondence course. For more details write to -

The Cartoon School

33 Saint Catherine's Road
Harrogate
HG2 8JZ